Contents

Let's Play!

Children everywhere play games. This book tells you about the games children play all over the world.

Old and new

Children often play old games their grandparents played. Other games are new.

Playing games is all about having fun.

Playground games around the world

es

J

BIG
PICTURE

Sarah Levete

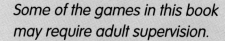

Some of the games in this book may require adult supervision.

Published 2010 by
A&C Black Publishers Ltd.
36 Soho Square, London, W1D 3QY

www.acblack.com

ISBN HB 978-1-4081-2799-5
      PB 978-1-4081-3161-9

This book is produced using paper that is made from wood grown in managed, sustainable forests. It is natural, renewable and recyclable. The logging and manufacturing processes conform to the environmental regulations of the country of origin.

Produced for A&C Black by Calcium. www.calciumcreative.co.uk

Printed and bound in China by C&C Offset Printing Co.

All the internet addresses given in this book were correct at the time of going to press. The author and publishers regret any inconvenience caused if addresses have changed or sites have ceased to exist, but can accept no responsibility for any such changes.

Acknowledgements

The publishers would like to thank the following for their kind permission to reproduce their photographs:

Cover: Shutterstock: Lucian Coman (front), Supri Suharjoto (back). **Pages:** Corbis: Image100 19; Fotolia: Poco_bw 4-5, Solaria 18; Istockphoto: Zhang Bo 10-11, Shawn Gearhart 20-21; Rex Features: Eye Ubiquitous 14, Novastock 16; Shutterstock: 9507848116 6, Rodolfo Arpia 13, Mags Ascough 14-15, Cheryl Casey 1, Lucian Coman 8-9, Mandy Godbehear 2-3, Iofoto 7, Lagui 21, Morgan Lane Photography 17, Philip Lange 6-7, Paul Maguire 18-19, Milos Markovic 10-11 (background), Michelle D. Milliman 12-13, Panaspics 12, Patrimonio Designs Limited 20, Antonio Petrone 16-17, Myron Pronyshyn 22-23, Supri Suharjoto 4, 24, Leah-Anne Thompson 8, Yuriy Kulyk 3.

Fun outdoors

Outdoor games are great!
You usually run around to play
them, which keeps you fit.

Have fun!

In the Air

From an orange to a rolled-up sock, you can use almost anything as a ball!

Keep it up!

Takraw is a ball game. Players try to keep the ball in the air without using their hands.

Fruit ball!

Clap Ball is a ball game played with grapefruits and oranges! You must catch the fruit, then clap your hands and stamp your feet.

Catch!

An apple makes a great ball!

Hop and Skip

Jumping and skipping games are often played to songs or rhymes.

Slide and hop

Tinikling is a game played with two **bamboo poles**. Two children slide the poles apart so another player can jump between them. They then close them together as he hops out.

You can play hop and skip games on your own!

Hop, hop, hop

S-t-r-e-t-ch!

Try this game called Lompat Tali.
1. Loop together lots of **elastic** bands
   to make a stretchy rope.
2. Two children hold the rope.
3. Another child jumps over the rope.

Chase Me!

There are lots of ways to play chase games. Often, one person tries to catch other players.

Who's it?

In chase games, the catcher is often called 'it'. Sometimes, children play a running game first to choose who will be 'it'.

When a player is caught, he or she becomes the chaser.

Snake chase

Big Snake is a chase game.
When people are caught,
they all join hands to form
a long snake. Sssssssss!

Can't catch me!

Hop to It!

Do you play Hopscotch? Children all over the world play this game.

How to play

To play Hopscotch, draw numbered squares on the ground. Start by throwing a stone into square 1, then hop over it onto the other squares.

You keep on throwing and hopping until you reach the last square.

Kangaroo Hop

Children in Australia play a game called Kangaroo Hop. The winner is the person who can hop the furthest.

Boing!

13

All a Board

Did you know that you can play board games **without a board?**

All you need...

Children all over the world play board games with just chalk, sticks, pebbles, and sand.

These children are playing a game with stones called Yote.

Play Yote!

1. Draw a square with six lines down and six across.
2. Each player has 12 stones lined up. Take it in turns to move them forwards, backwards, left, or right.
3. You take the other person's stones by jumping over them into an empty space.

Your go...

Toss and Roll

Stones, glass balls, plastic balls –
you can toss them in the air or
roll them on the ground.

Marbles

Draw a chalk circle on
the ground. Put one
marble in the middle.
Try to hit it with
another marble.

*The person who hits
the marble first wins.*

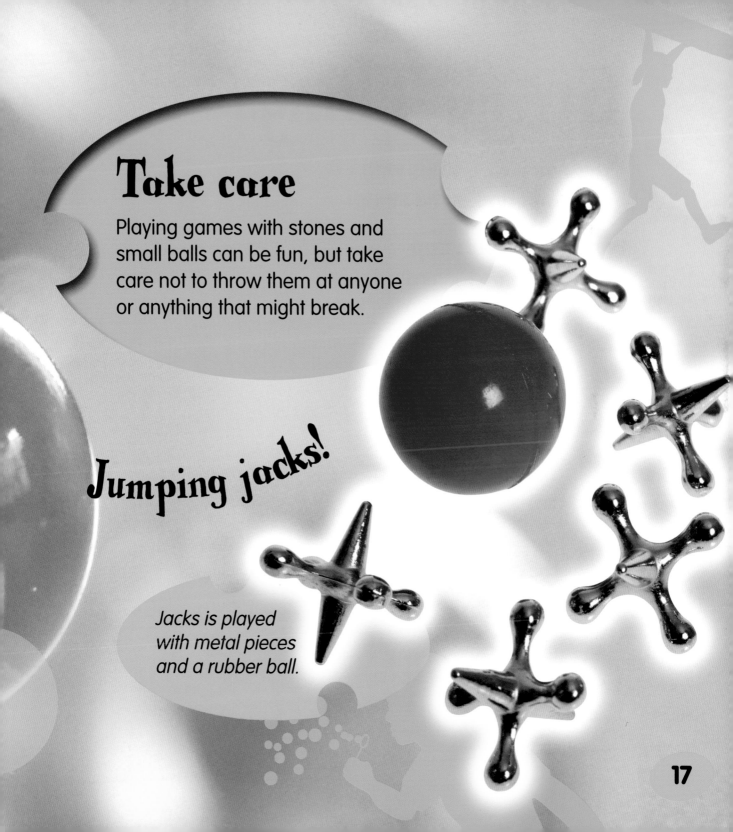

Take care

Playing games with stones and small balls can be fun, but take care not to throw them at anyone or anything that might break.

Jumping jacks!

Jacks is played with metal pieces and a rubber ball.

String Things

You can play games with just a nut and some string!

Catch it in the cup

To play Bolero, children tie a cup and ball to a string, then fix the string to a stick. The aim of the game is to toss the ball into the cup.

Bolero takes a lot of practice to play.

It's nuts!

Children tie a **conker** to a piece of string to play Conkers. They hit another child's conker. The player whose conker doesn't smash is the winner.

Smash!

19

A Long Story

Here are some fun stories about how games began...

Tug of war

People in China once believed that the Sun and Moon played Tug of War.

Heeeaaave!

Roman soldiers played Hopscotch in **armour** to train for war!

Sore loser

Many years ago people called **Aztecs** played a game like basketball. It was important to win – losers were killed!

Glossary

armour tough, metal coverings people wore to protect their body in battle

Aztecs people who lived in South America a long time ago

bamboo a tropical plant with a hard, hollow stem

board games games played using a board and counters

conker a hard, brown nut

elastic a stretchy material

marble a small, hard ball

poles long, straight sticks

Further Reading

Websites

Find out more about playground games at:
www.playgroundfun.org.uk

Get lots of ideas for great games at:
**www.woodlands-junior.kent.sch.uk/studentssite/
playgroundgames.htm**

There are lots of play ideas at:

kids.activedmonton.ca/Game_rules/int

Books

Games (Around the World) by
Margaret C. Hall, Heinemann (2003).

Hopscotch (Start Reading: Fun and Games)
by Anna Matthew, Wayland (2009).

Play With Us by Oriol Ripoll, Chicago Review
Press (2005).

Index